THE WORLD IS ONE BIG ORGY

TARNOWSKI   SALTER

To order additional copies of this book, contact:
Xlibris
1-888-795-4274
www.Xlibris.com
Orders@Xlibris.com

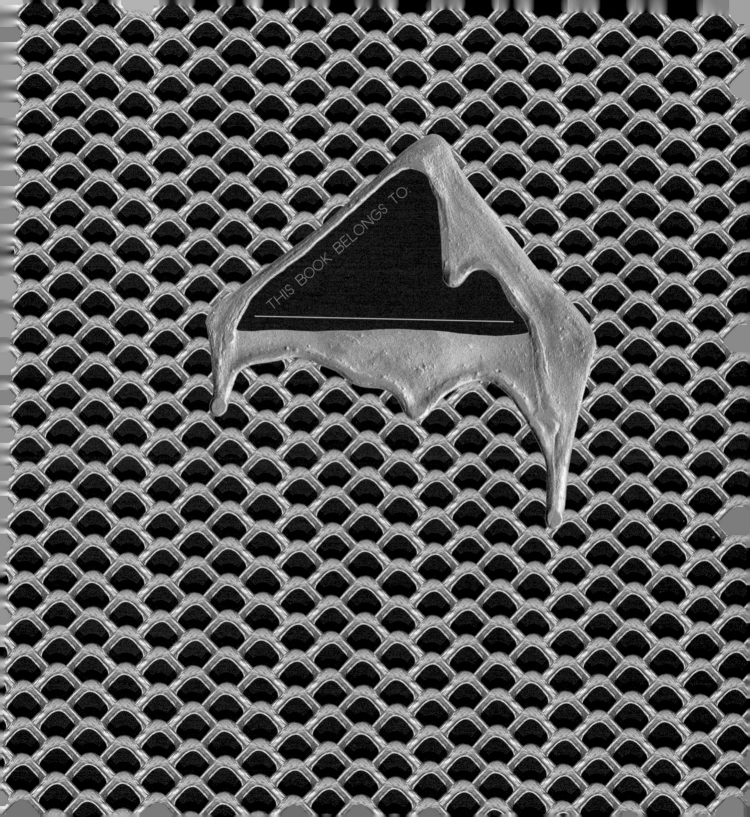

THIS BOOK BELONGS TO:

WARNING!!!
THIS BOOK MAY
LOOK CUTE BUT
IT IS **NOT!** IT IS
VULGAR AND
NOT INTENDED
FOR **ANY**
CHILDREN... **EVER!**

DEDICATED TO :
**KATE, CALI MAN, MANTHA, EMILY, RONAN, LEO
AND LUKE**

THANK YOU FOR BELIEVING THAT WE COULD
MAKE SOMETHING SILLY AND PERVERTED, YET
SOMEHOW STILL MEANINGFUL

THE WORLD IS ONE BIG ORGY

TARNOWSKI   SALTER

THE BEGINNING...

THERE WAS THIS BIG...

BRAAAA

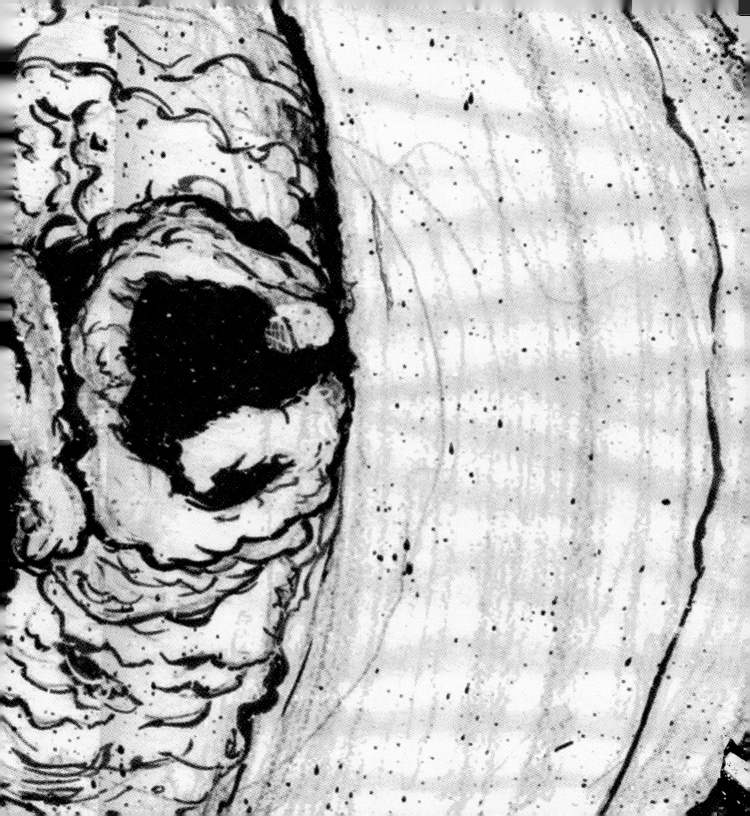

This created the Universe

From This Big bang

ON THE EARTH THE ATMOSPHER
LLOWED THE CREATION OF WATER, AND WATER
CREATED PLANT LIFE AND TREES, WHICH
CREATED OXYGEN

LIVING IN THE WATER WERE MICROSCOPIC

ORGANISMS

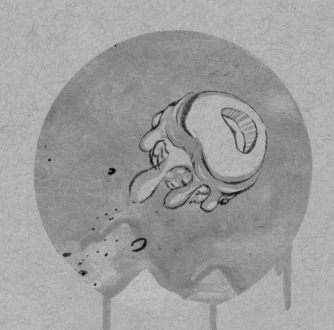

THESE NEW ORGANISMS BANGED OTHER NEW ORGANISMS
THAT WERE JUST A LITTLE BIT DIFFERENT, AND THESE
CREATED WEIRD NEW, BIGGER ORGANISMS

AFTER HUNDREDS OF THOUSANDS OF YEARS OF SEXING U
M

MICROSCOPIC. AND CREATING NEW WEIRD CREATURES. WE HAVE FISH

THIS FISH FUCKED THIS FISH, WHICH MADE THIS WEIRD FISH

THOUSANDS OF WEIRD FISH FUCKEDOTHER WEIRD FISH

CREATION WENT O

NOW WE HAVE ALL SORTS OF NEW CREATURES
PORKING EACH OTHER AND CREATING NEW WEIRD SHIT
LIKE the PLATYPUS.

THIS WAY. WEIRD ANIMALS FUCKING OTHER WEIRD ANIMAL

SOME ANIMALS HAVE COME AND GONE LIKE THE DINOSAURS

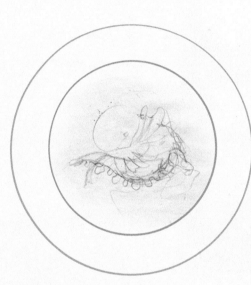

WHATEVER ANIMALS SCREWED TO CREATE THOSE ARE OBVIOUSLY GONE BECAUSE WE DON'T HAVE THEM TODAY

THAT SHIT WOULD BE CRAY CRAY

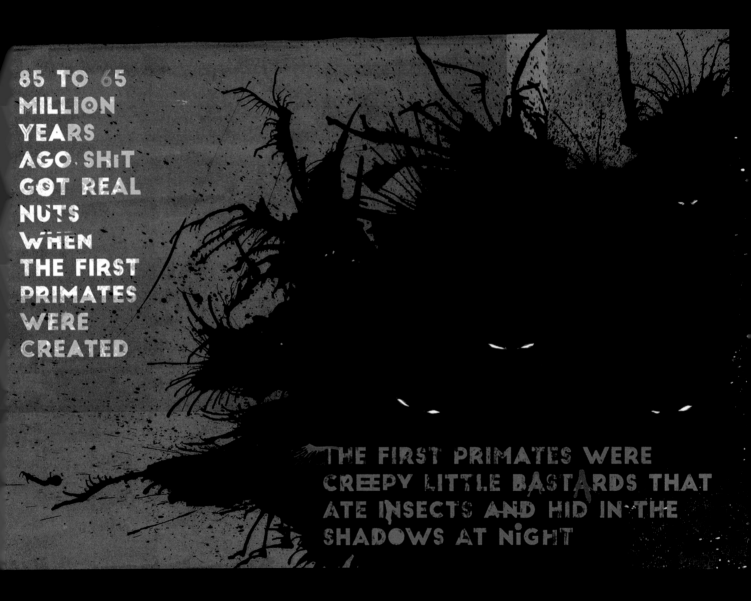

85 TO 65 MILLION YEARS AGO SHIT GOT REAL NUTS WHEN THE FIRST PRIMATES WERE CREATED

THE FIRST PRIMATES WERE CREEPY LITTLE BASTARDS THAT ATE INSECTS AND HID IN THE SHADOWS AT NIGHT

THEY WERE NOT VERY BIG, BUT AS WE LEARNED FROM THE
DINOSAURS, YOU FUCK ENOUGH WEIRD SHIT AND YOU QUIT
POSSIBLY WILL MAKE SOMETHING BIG AND SCARY

HAT WAS EXACTLY WHAT HAPPENED 70 OR SO MILLION
YEARS OF DIRTY TREE SHREW AND LEMUR PORN
WE HAD   THE FIRST OF

HESE BIG BEAUTIFUL GREAT APES ARE THE CLOSEST LINK TO

EVEN CLOSER TO U

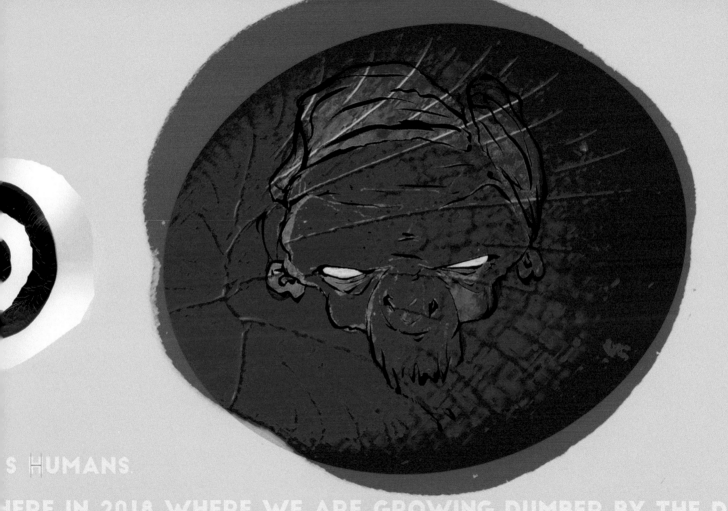

S HUMANS.

HERE IN 2018. WHERE WE ARE GROWING DUMBER BY THE DA

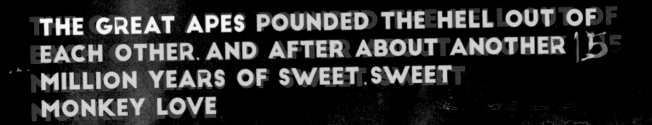

THE GREAT APES POUNDED THE HELL OUT OF
EACH OTHER. AND AFTER ABOUT ANOTHER 15
MILLION YEARS OF SWEET, SWEET
MONKEY LOVE

WE HAD   THE FIRST
HOMOSAPIENS

AND ALL WAS RIGHT IN THE WORLD WITH GLORIOUS DREAMS OF FORTUNES UNTOLD.

SMOG AND
EVENTUALLY
DIMENTIA

IN 776 B.C. THE FIRST OLYMPIC GAMES WERE HELD

IN 56ºA.D. WE INVENTED Fellatio

WE CREATED GREAT PYRAMIDS AND GREAT WALLS

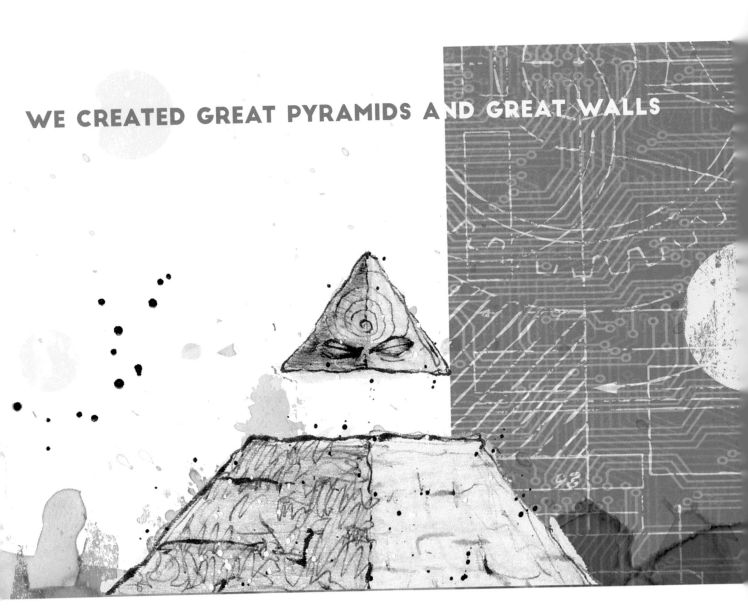

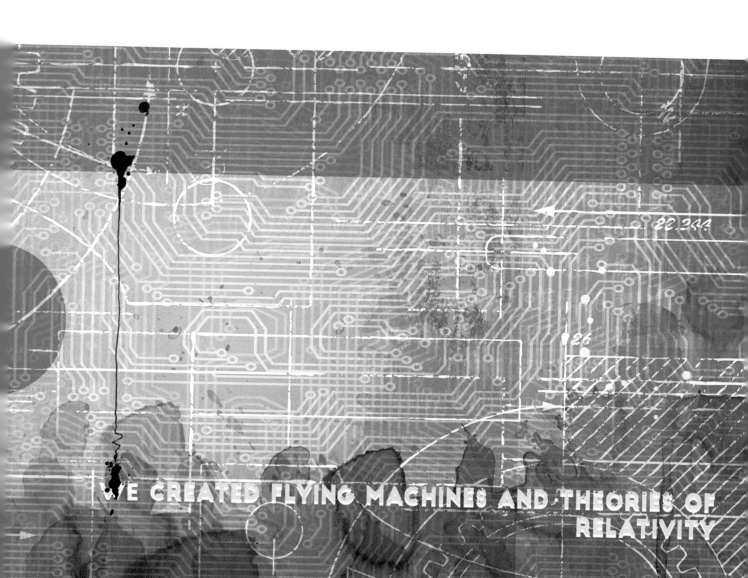

WE CREATED FLYING MACHINES AND THEORIES OF RELATIVITY

WE FOUGHT WARS FOR THINGS WE BELIEVED IN
AND EVEN SOME THINGS WE DIDNT BELIEVE IN

WE HAVE ELECTED FREE THINKERS, PATRIOTS, MONSTERS, WAR MONGERS AND CARROTS.

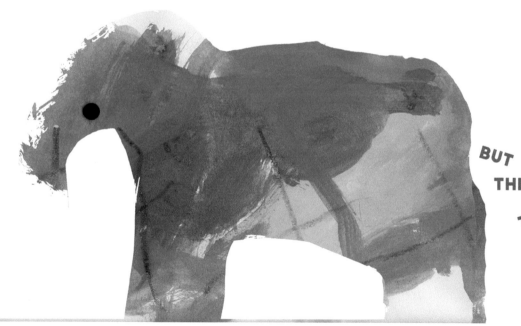

BUT
THE BEST
THING
WE HAVE
EVER CREATED...

IS EACH OTHER!

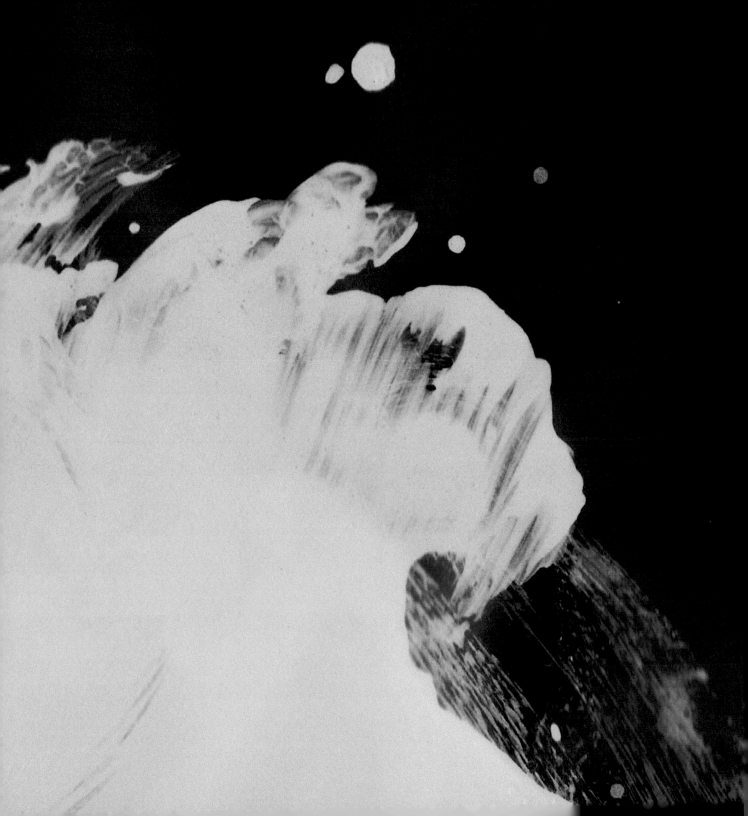

THIS WORLD COULD
USE A LITTLE **COLOR**

go for it!!

WORD HUNT

```
C A R R O T M P A P
A M O E B A U P M I
P E P E T P S V O P
M B V M R H B R O R
P O R G A S M R P R G
L I V E A R T H H G
P U R G E T O R O A
O M V T A G O A U N
P H A P P Y P P S I
P L A T Y P U S P S
M F E L L A T I O M
```

PLATYPUS
AMOEBA
AMORPHOUS
ORGANISM
MUSH
FELLATIO
HAPPY
LOVE
CARROT
PURGE

CONNECT THF **DOTS**

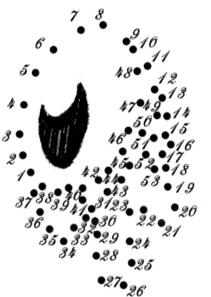

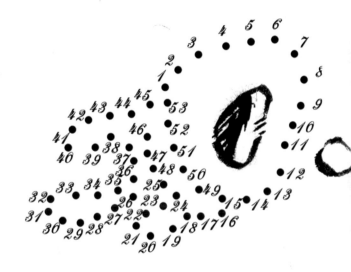

IN THE STUDIO

SPRINKLER
VALVE INSIDE

DANGER

Open Slowly

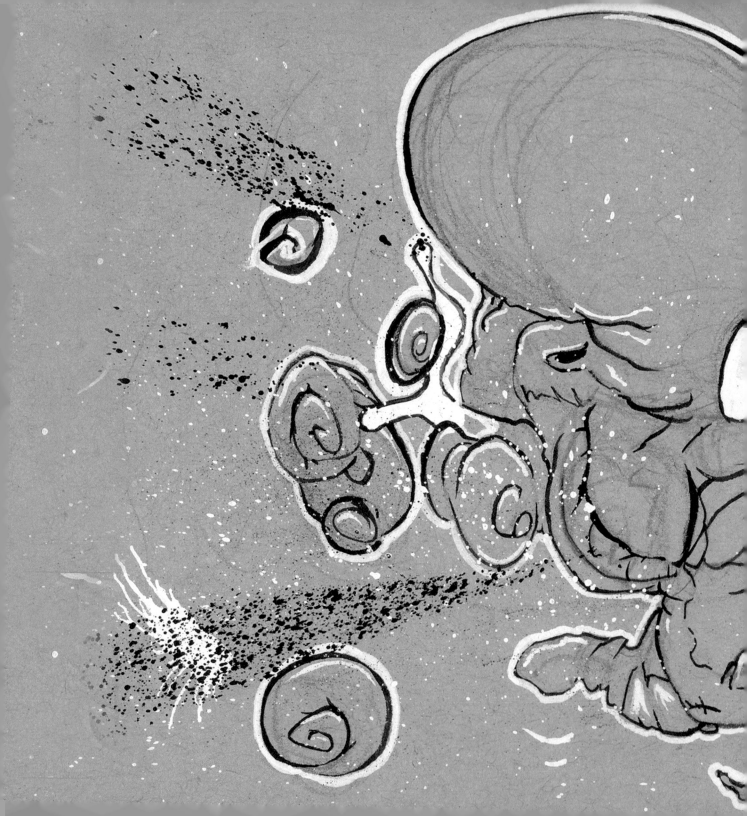

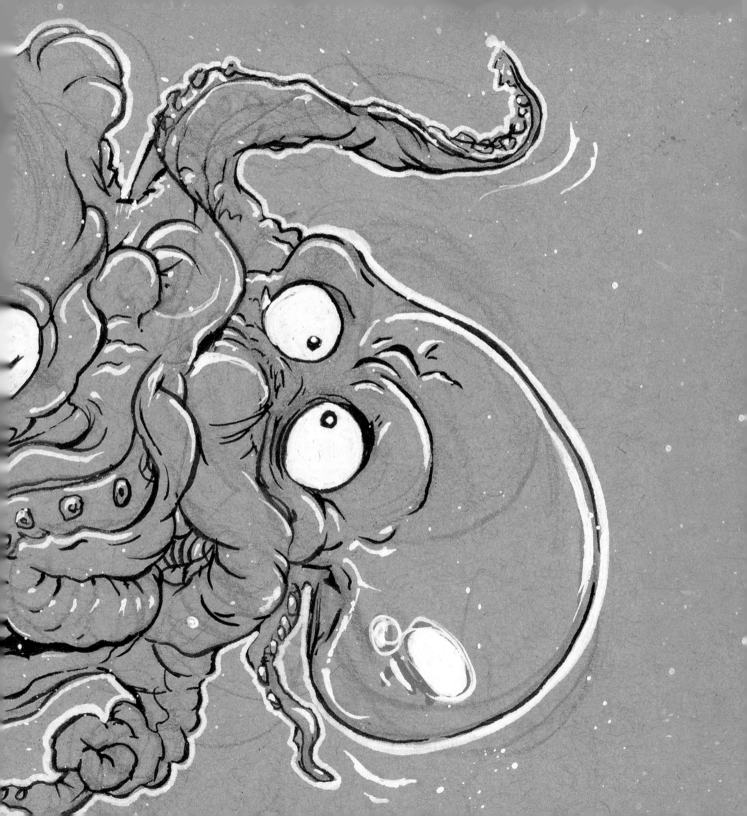

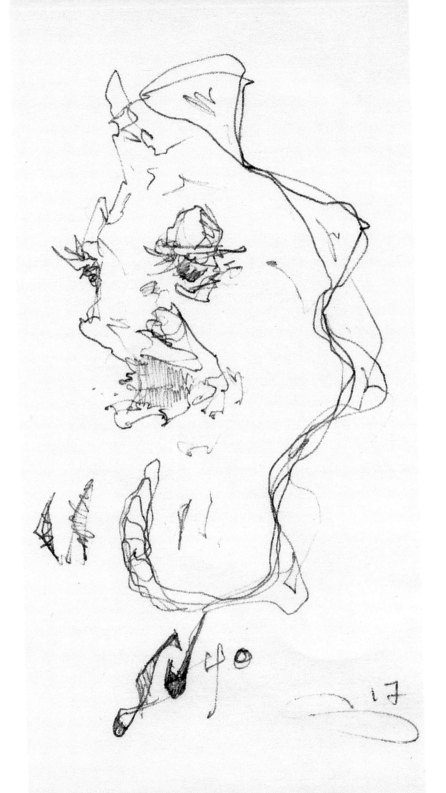

FINALLY THERE BECAME FEW THAT I

Printed in the United States
By Bookmasters